200 cocktails

hamlyn | all colour cookbook

200 cocktails

An Hachette UK Company
www.hachette.co.uk

First published in Great Britain in 2008 by Hamlyn,
a division of Octopus Publishing Group Ltd
Endeavour House, 189 Shaftesbury Avenue,
London WC2H 8JY
www.octopusbooks.co.uk

ISBN: 978-0-600-61020-5

A CIP catalogue record for this book is available from the
British Library

Printed and bound in China

6 7 8 9 10

The measure that has been used in the recipes is based
on a bar jigger, which is 25 ml (1 fl oz). If preferred, a
different volume can be used, providing the proportions are
kept constant within a drink and suitable adjustments are
made to spoon measurements, where they occur.

Standard level spoon measurements are used in all recipes.
1 tablespoon = one 15 ml spoon
1 teaspoon = one 5 ml spoon

The Department of Health advises that eggs should not be
consumed raw. This book contains some recipes made with
raw eggs. It is prudent for vulnerable people such as
pregnant and nursing mothers, invalids and the elderly to
avoid these recipes.

This book includes recipes made with nuts and nut
derivatives. It is advisable for those with known allergic
reactions to nuts and nut derivatives to avoid these recipes.
It is also prudent to check the labels of pre-prepared
ingredients for the possible inclusion of nut derivatives.

The UK Health Department recommends that men do not
regularly exceed 3–4 units a day and women 2–3 units a day,
a unit being defined as 10 ml of pure alcohol, the equivalent
of a single measure (25 ml) of spirits. Those who regularly
drink more than this run an increasingly significant risk of
illness and death from a number of conditions. In addition,
women who are pregnant or trying to conceive should avoid
drinking alcohol.

contents

introduction

What's in a cocktail?

The word cocktail conjures up all sorts of images, mainly associated with celebrations, entertaining and enjoyment. A cocktail is essentially a mixed drink with a spirit base (usually gin, vodka, whisky, rum or tequila) that is combined with tonic, juice or another non-alcoholic mixer. Often a third ingredient is added, a flavouring to complement the spirit and add a distinctive flavour. This can be anything from a sugar cube to Angostura bitters.

From humble beginnings

There are several theories about the origins of the cocktail, some more credible than others. It has been suggested that the name was adapted from the French word *coquetier*, meaning egg cup, in which the first cocktail – the Sazerac – was originally served. It's also been said that the word came from a tavern in New York where the innkeeper's daughter made a drink for her intended on his return from a sailing expedition. He brought back a fighting cockerel, and the daughter used its tail feathers to decorate his drink. But many think that the cocktail came into being in the United States the 1920s, during Prohibition. The banning of alcohol forced people to seek out interesting ways of flavouring the infamous bathtub gin and other bootleg liquors.

Choosing glasses

There are thousands of different cocktails, but they all fall into one of three categories: long, short or shot. Long drinks generally have more mixer than alcohol and are often served with ice and a straw. The terms 'straight up' and 'on the rocks' are synonymous with the short drink, which tends to be more about the spirit, which is often combined with a single mixer, at most. Finally, there is the shot. These miniature cocktails are made up mainly from spirits and liqueurs and are designed to give a quick hit of alcohol. Cocktail glasses are tailored to the type of drinks they will contain.

Champagne flute
Used for Champagne or Champagne cocktails, the narrow mouth of the flute helps the drink to stay fizzy.

Champagne saucer
These old-fashioned glasses are not very practical for serving Champagne because the drink quickly loses its fizz.

Wine glass
Sangria (see page 96) is often served in a wine glass, but they are not usually used for cocktails.

Martini glass
A martini glass, also known as a cocktail glass, is designed so that your hand can't warm the glass, making sure that the cocktail is served completely chilled.

Margarita or coupette glass
When this type of glass is used for a Margarita, the rim is dipped in salt. These glasses are used for daiquiris and other fruit-based cocktails.

Highball glass
A highball glass is suitable for any long cocktail, from the Cuba Libre (see page 78) to Long Island Iced Tea (see page 92).

Old-fashioned glass
Also known as a rocks glass, the old-fashioned glass is great for any drink that's served on the rocks or straight up. It's also good for muddled drinks.

Shot glass
Shot glasses are often found in two sizes — for a single or double measure. They are ideal for a single mouthful, which can range from a Tequila Shot (see page 230) to the more decadent layered B-52 (see page 224).

Balloon glass
These glasses are usually used for fine spirits, whose aroma is as important as the taste. The glass can be warmed to encourage the release of the aroma.

Hurricane glass
This type of glass is mostly found in beach bars, where it is used to serve creamy, rum-based drinks.

Boston glass
Often used by bartenders for mixing cocktails, the Boston glass is also good for fruity drinks.

Toddy glass
A toddy glass is generally used for a hot drink, such as Irish Coffee.

Setting up the bar

Useful equipment
There are a few tools that are worth investing in if you are planning to make cocktails.

Shaker
The Boston shaker is the most simple option, but it needs to be used in conjunction with a hawthorne strainer. Alternatively you could choose a shaker with a built-in strainer.

Mixing glass
A mixing glass is used for those drinks that require only a gentle stirring before they are poured or strained.

Food processor
A food processor or blender is useful for making frozen cocktails and smoothies.

Hawthorne strainer
This type of strainer is often used in conjunction with a Boston shaker, but a tea strainer will also work well.

Muddling stick
Similar to a pestle, which will work just as well, a muddling stick, or muddler, is used to crush fruit or herbs in a glass or shaker for drinks like the Mojito (see page 76).

Bar spoon
Similar to a teaspoon but with a long handle, a bar spoon is used for stirring, layering and muddling drinks.

Measure or jigger
Single and double measures are available and are essential when you are mixing ingredients so that the proportions are always the same. One measure is 25 ml or 1 fl oz.

Bottle opener
Some bottle openers have two attachments, one for metal-topped bottles and a corkscrew for wine bottles.

Pourers
A pourer is inserted into the top of a spirit bottle to enable the spirit to flow in a controlled manner.

The spirits and their partners

Each spirit has a natural affinity with certain flavours, and it is from these complementary relationships that cocktails are born.

Brandy

Much brandy is distilled from grapes, but there are some varieties that use other fruits as their base. Serve brandy with fruit and fruit juices, but don't use the finest brandies for mixed drinks.

Gin

A clear grain spirit infused with juniper berries, gin was first produced in Holland over 400 years ago. Serve it with citrus fruits, fresh berries and tonic water.

Rum

This Caribbean staple, which dates back to the 17th century, is made from sugar cane left over after sugar production. Serve rum with any of the exotic fruits, cream or cola.

Tequila

Mexico's best-known spirit is made from the blue agave plant, and its origins can be traced back to the Aztecs. It was traditionally served by itself as a Tequila Slammer (see page 216), but also works well with citrus and sour fruits as well as ginger and tomato.

Vodka

Vodka is distilled from grain and is relatively free from natural flavour. There is fierce debate as to its origins, with both the Poles and the Russians claiming to have invented the drink. With its neutral character, it is infinitely mixable with a huge range of flavours. Serve it with cranberry, tomato or citrus juices, or for a classic drink simply add tonic water.

Whisky

The origins of whisky are hotly debated, with both Scotland and Ireland staking a claim to having developed it. Modern whiskies have a much smoother taste and texture, and there are two main types: blended and unblended. Serve it with water, soda water, cola or ginger ale.

Sugar syrup

This is used as a sweetener in lots of cocktails. It blends into a cold drink more quickly than sugar and adds body. You can buy this in bottles, but it's very easy to make your own. Simply bring equal quantities of caster sugar and water to the boil in a small saucepan, stirring continuously, then boil for 1–2 minutes without stirring. Sugar syrup can be kept in a sterilised bottle in the refrigerator for up to 2 months.

Perfecting your technique

With just a few basic techniques, your bartending skills will be complete. Follow the step-by-step instructions to hone your craft and mix perfect cocktails.

Blending

Frozen cocktails and smoothies are blended with ice in a blender until they are of a smooth consistency. A frozen Daiquiri or Margarita is made using a virtually identical recipe to the unfrozen versions but with a scoop of crushed ice added to the blender before blending on high speed. Be careful not to add too much ice to the recipe as this will dilute the cocktail. It's best to add a little at a time.

Muddling

Muddling is a technique that is used to bring out the flavours of herbs and fruit using a blunt tool called a muddler, and the best-known muddled drink is the Mojito (see page 76).
1 Add mint leaves to a highball glass. Add some sugar syrup and some lime wedges.
2 Hold the glass firmly and use a muddler or pestle to press down. Twist and press to release the flavours.
3 Continue this for about 30 seconds, then top up the glass with crushed ice and add the remaining ingredients.

Shaking

The best-known cocktail technique and probably the one that you use most often, so it's important to get right. Shaking is used to mix ingredients quickly and thoroughly, and to chill the drink before serving.
1 Half-fill a cocktail shaker with ice cubes, or cracked or crushed ice.
2 If the recipe calls for a chilled glass add a few ice cubes and some cold water to the glass, swirl it around and discard.
3 Add the recipe ingredients to the shaker and shake until a frost forms on the outside. Use both hands, one at each end, so that it doesn't slip.
4 Strain the cocktail into the glass and serve.

Layering

A number of spirits can be served layered on top of each other, and because some spirits are lighter than others they will float on top of your cocktail.

1 Pour the first ingredient into a glass, taking care that it does not touch the sides.

2 Position a bar spoon in the centre of the glass, rounded part down and facing you. Rest the spoon against the side of the glass as your pour the second ingredient down the spoon. It should float on top of the first liquid, creating a separate layer.

3 Repeat with the third ingredient, then carefully remove the spoon.

Building

This is a straightforward technique that involves nothing more than putting the ingredients together in the correct order.

1 Have all the ingredients for the cocktail to hand. Chill the glass, if required.

2 Add each ingredient in recipe order, making sure that all measures are exact.

Double-straining

When you want to prevent all traces of puréed fruit and ice fragments from entering the glass, use a shaker with a built-in strainer in conjunction with a hawthorne strainer. Alternatively, strain through a fine strainer.

Stirring

A cocktail is prepared by stirring when the ingredients need to be mixed and chilled but it's important to maintain the clarity. This ensures that there is no fragmented ice or air bubbles throughout the drink. Some stirred cocktails will require the ingredients to be prepared in a mixing glass, then strained into the serving glass with a fine strainer.

1 Add the ingredients to a glass in the order stated in the recipe.

2 Use a bar spoon to stir the drink, lightly or vigorously, as described in the recipe.

3 Finish the drink with any decoration and serve.

The finishing touches

Some cocktails are decorated for decoration's sake, but in others the decoration is a vital part of the flavour — the green olive in a Dry Martini, for example. Decorations can range from a simple twist of lemon to a complicated assemblage of fruit on a cocktail stick. The possibilities are almost endless, ranging from celery sticks, slices of cucumber, cracked pepper and cherry tomatoes to prawns and even quails' eggs.

Wedges

Citrus fruits work well as wedges. The wedge can be squeezed into the drink then dropped in or served on the rim of the glass. Simply slide a sharp knife through the flesh so that you can balance it on the rim.

Slices

Any round fruit, such as kiwifruit, limes, lemons, oranges and apples, can be cut into cross-sections to create a slice. You can either place the slice on the rim of the glass or float it on the surface of the drink. Use your imagination and take your inspiration from the flavours in the cocktail.

Twists

Citrus twists not only look good but also impart flavour to the cocktail. Pare a strip of rind from the fruit and remove all signs of pith. Twist the rind over the surface of the drink to release the oils, then drop it into the drink. Flaming the rind before twisting it releases even more flavour.

Spirals

Citrus spirals look great when they are draped over the side of the drink or dropped into it. Use a cannelle knife to cut a long, thin strip of rind from the fruit and wind it around a cylinder, such as a bar spoon, straw or swizzle stick, to create a spiral. Hold it for a few seconds to allow it to set into shape.

Fruit kebabs

Miniature kebabs can be balanced on top of drinks or placed in them. Try a combination of berries in descending order of size, such as

a strawberry, blackberry, raspberry and blueberry, or use fruit of matching colours. Another option is to pick out fruits that feature in the flavouring of the cocktail. Simply thread them on to a cocktail stick.

Herbs

Sprigs of herbs make attractive and fragrant decorations. They can be used to decorate the glass or used in the drink, as in the Virginia Mint Julep (see page 88).

Novelty decorations

There are a number of novelty decorations that are not as popular as they once were, but can still look great with the right cocktail, especially when served at a themed party. Paper umbrellas, plastic monkeys and even sparklers are just a few of the options available to liven up your drinks.

Frosting

Although it is not strictly a decoration, frosting a glass does add a very professional finishing touch to a drink. Frosting can add flavour, as in the salt used for the Margarita (see page 138), or it can be just visual, as with some sugar frostings.

To add a frosting, dip the rim of the glass in a saucer of lime or lemon juice or water. Spread the sugar or salt on a small plate and place the rim of the glass in the frosting. Twist to give an even coating and use a lime or lemon wedge to clean off any excess frosting from inside of the glass to preventing it contaminating the cocktail. If you want to be sure that the frosting will stay in place, use egg white in place of the citrus juice to stick the sugar or salt to the glass.

fabulously
fruity

sea breeze

makes **2**
glasses **2 highball glasses**
equipment **straws**

ice cubes
2 measures **vodka**
4 measures **cranberry juice**
2 measures **grapefruit juice**
lime wedges, to decorate

Fill 2 highball glasses with ice cubes, pour over the vodka, cranberry juice and grapefruit juice and stir well.

Decorate with lime wedges and serve.

For a Bay Breeze, a sweeter drink, replace the grapefruit juice with pineapple juice, which contrasts well with the slightly bitter taste of the cranberry juice.

storm at sea

makes **2**
glasses **2 old-fashioned glasses**
equipment **cocktail shaker, strainer**

4 measures **cranberry juice**
2 measures **pineapple juice**
4 teaspoons **elderflower cordial**
16–20 **ice cubes**
3 measures **Blavod vodka**

Put the cranberry juice, pineapple juice and elderflower cordial into a cocktail shaker with half the ice cubes and shake to mix, then strain into old-fashioned glasses over the remaining ice cubes.

Add the vodka slowly, which will separate briefly, and serve immediately.

For a Cape Codder, to serve 1, a longer, more refreshing drink, squeeze 6 lime wedges into a highball glass full of ice, add 2 measures of vodka and top up with cranberry juice.

sex on the beach

makes **2**
glasses **2 highball glasses**
equipment **cocktail shaker,
strainer**

ice cubes
2 measures **vodka**
2 measures **peach schnapps**
2 measures **cranberry juice**
2 measures **orange juice**
2 measures **pineapple juice**
(optional)
lemon and lime wedges,
to decorate

Put 8–10 ice cubes into a cocktail shaker and add the vodka, schnapps, cranberry juice, orange juice and pineapple juice (if used). Shake well.

Put 3–4 ice cubes into each highball glass, strain over the cocktail and decorate with the lemon and lime wedges.

For Sex in the Dunes, a shorter drink with more of a kick, replace the cranberry juice and orange juice with 1 measure of Chambord, shake well and decorate each glass with pineapple chunks.

marguerite

makes **2**

glasses **2 old-fashioned glasses**

equipment **cocktail shaker, strainer**

ice cubes, plus cracked ice to serve

6 measures **vodka**

juice of **2 lemons**

juice of **1 orange**

raspberry syrup, maraschino liqueur or grenadine, to taste

Put 8–10 ice cubes into a cocktail shaker. Pour the vodka, fruit juices and raspberry syrup, maraschino liqueur or grenadine over the ice. Shake until a frost forms on the outside of the shaker.

Strain into 2 old-fashioned glasses filled with cracked ice.

For a Screwdriver, one of the classic cocktails, use 1 measure of vodka to 2 measures fresh orange juice and serve over ice.

rising sun

makes **2**
glasses **2 old-fashioned
glasses**
equipment **cocktail shaker,
strainer**

ice cubes
4 measures **vodka**
4 teaspoons **passion fruit
syrup**
6 measures **grapefruit juice**
ruby grapefruit slices,
to decorate

Half-fill a cocktail shaker with ice cubes and put
6–8 ice cubes into each old-fashioned glass.

Add all the remaining ingredients to the shaker and
shake until a frost forms on the outside of the shaker.
Strain over the ice in the glasses, decorate each with
a ruby grapefruit slice and serve.

For a Harvey Wallbanger, a '60s cocktail inspired
by the Screwdriver, float a teaspoon of Galliano, the
Italian herb-flavoured liqueur, over a mixture of
1 measure of vodka and 3 measures of orange
juice and plenty of ice.

green island fragrance

makes **2**

glasses **2 highball glasses**

equipment **cocktail shaker, strainer, straws**

3 measures **vodka**

1 measure **Midori**

2 measures **lemon juice**

2 measures **pineapple juice**

2 dashes **sugar syrup**

ice cubes, plus crushed ice to serve

2 **lemon wedges**

Put the vodka, Midori, lemon juice and pineapple juice into a cocktail shaker and add the sugar syrup and some ice cubes. Put some crushed ice into the highball glasses.

Shake and strain over the ice into the glasses. Squeeze a lemon wedge over each drink, then drop it into the glass, and serve with straws.

For a Vodka Caipiroska, to serve 1, muddle together 6 lime wedges with 2 teaspoons of light brown sugar in an old-fashioned glass, then add 2 measures of vodka and top up with crushed ice.

laila cocktail

makes **2**

glasses **2 chilled martini
glasses**

equipment **muddling stick,
cocktail shaker, strainer,
cocktail sticks**

4 **lime wedges**

4 **strawberries**

8 **blueberries**, plus extra to
decorate

2 dashes **mango purée**

2 measures **raspberry vodka**

ice cubes

Muddle the lime wedges, berries and mango purée in
the bottom of a cocktail shaker.

Add the raspberry vodka and some ice cubes and
shake vigorously. Double-strain into 2 chilled martini
glasses, decorate with 3 extra blueberries on a cocktail
stick and serve.

For a Rock Chick, which uses another fruit vodka,
shake together 2 measures of blackcurrant vodka with
a generous dash of peach schnapps and lime juice
and plenty of ice. Strain into 2 chilled martini glasses.

gin garden martini

makes **2**

glasses **2 chilled martini glasses**

equipment **muddling stick, cocktail shaker, strainer**

½ **cucumber**, peeled and chopped, plus extra slices to decorate

1 measure **elderflower cordial**

4 measures **gin**

2 measures **pressed apple juice**

ice cubes

Muddle the cucumber in the bottom of a cocktail shaker with the elderflower cordial.

Add the gin, apple juice and some ice cubes. Shake and double-strain into 2 chilled martini glasses, decorate with peeled cucumber slices and serve.

For an Apple Martini, mix 4 measures of vodka, 2 measures of apple schnapps and 2 tablespoons of apple purée in a cocktail shaker with plenty of ice cubes. Add a generous dash of lime juice and a pinch of ground cinnamon, shake and strain into 2 chilled martini glasses decorated with red apple wedges.

valentine martini

makes **2**

glasses **2 chilled martini glasses**

equipment **cocktail shaker, strainer, cocktail sticks**

ice cubes

4 measures **raspberry vodka**

12 **raspberries,** plus extra to decorate

1 measure **lime juice**

2 dashes **sugar syrup**

lime rind spirals, to decorate

Half-fill a cocktail shaker with ice cubes. Add all the remaining ingredients and shake until a frost forms on the outside of the shaker. Double-strain into 2 chilled martini glasses.

Decorate with the extra raspberries and a lime rind spiral on cocktail sticks and serve.

For a Watermelon Martini, squeeze the juice of half a lime into a cocktail shaker, add 8 chunks of watermelon, 3 measures of vodka, 1 measure of passion fruit liqueur and a dash of cranberry juice. Shake over ice then strain into 2 chilled martini glasses and decorate with a watermelon wedge.

papa doble

makes **2**
glasses **2 highball glasses**
equipment **food processor**

crushed ice
6 measures **white rum**
1 measure **maraschino liqueur**
2 measures **lime juice**
3 measures **grapefruit juice**
grapefruit slices,
   to decorate

Put a scoop of crushed ice into a food processor or blender with the rum, maraschino and fruit juices and blend until smooth.

Serve in 2 highball glasses with half grapefruit slices. This drink can be sweetened to taste with sugar syrup, although Hemingway, after whom this drink was named, never would have done so.

For a Cooper Cooler, another rum drink from the Caribbean, fill an old-fashioned glass with plenty of ice, add 2 measures of golden rum and a dash of lime juice and top up with ginger ale.

red rum

makes **2**

glasses **2 chilled martini glasses**

equipment **muddling stick, cocktail shaker, strainer**

handful of **redcurrants**, plus extra to decorate

1 measure **sloe gin**

4 measures **Bacardi 8-year-old rum**

1 measure **lemon juice**

1 measure **vanilla syrup**

ice cubes

Muddle the redcurrants and sloe gin together in the bottom of a cocktail shaker.

Add the rum, lemon juice and vanilla syrup and some ice cubes.

Shake and double-strain into 2 chilled martini glasses, decorate with some redcurrants and serve.

For a Rude Jude, another delectable fruity concoction, put 2 measures of white rum and a generous dash each of strawberry syrup, strawberry purée and lime juice into a cocktail shaker with plenty of ice. Shake and strain into 2 chilled martini glasses.

pineapple mojito

makes **2**

glasses **2 highball glasses**

equipment **muddling stick, cocktail shaker, strainer**

1 **lime**

12 **mint leaves**, plus extra to decorate

8 **pineapple chunks**, plus wedges to decorate

4 teaspoons **brown sugar**

4 measures **golden rum**

crushed ice

pineapple juice, to top up

Cut the lime into wedges and muddle with the mint, pineapple chunks and sugar in the bottom of a cocktail shaker. Add the rum and shake with crushed ice.

Pour into 2 highball glasses, top up with crushed ice and pineapple juice and stir. Decorate with a pineapple wedge and a mint sprig.

For a Pink Mojito, to serve 1, muddle 6 mint leaves, the juice of half a lime, 2 teaspoons of sugar syrup and 3 raspberries in a highball glass. Add a handful of crushed ice, then pour in 1½ measures of white rum and ½ measure of Chambord. Stir well, then top up with cranberry juice and decorate with mint sprigs.

strawberry daiquiri

makes **1**

glasses **1 chilled martini glass**

equipment **muddling stick, cocktail shaker, strainer**

3 **strawberries**, hulled

dash of **strawberry syrup**

6 **mint leaves**, plus a sprig to decorate

2 measures **golden rum**

2 measures **lime juice**

strawberry slice, to decorate

Muddle the strawberries, syrup and mint leaves in the bottom of a cocktail shaker.

Add the rum and lime juice, shake with ice and double-strain into a chilled martini glass. Decorate with a strawberry slice and a sprig of mint.

For a Melon Daiquiri, to serve 1, shake 2 measures of rum, 1 measure of lime juice and ½ measure of Midori with plenty of crushed ice, then strain into a chilled martini glass. Decorate with a small wedge of melon.

moon river

makes **2**

glasses **2 chilled martini glasses**

equipment **cocktail shaker, strainer**

ice cubes
1 measure **dry gin**
1 measure **apricot brandy**
1 measure **Cointreau**
½ measure **Galliano**
½ measure **lemon juice**
maraschino cherries,
  to decorate

Put some ice cubes into a cocktail shaker. Pour the gin, apricot brandy, Cointreau, Galliano and lemon juice over the ice.

Shake, then strain into 2 large chilled martini glasses. Decorate each with a cherry.

For a Maiden's Prayer, pour 4 measures of gin into a cocktail shaker with some ice, add 4 measures of Cointreau and 2 measures of orange juice. Shake well, then strain into 2 chilled martini glasses.

orange blossom

makes **2**
glasses **2 highball glasses**
equipment **muddling stick,
  straws**

8 **orange slices**, plus wedges
  to decorate
4 teaspoons **almond syrup**
crushed ice
4 measures **gin**
2 measures **pink grapefruit
  juice**
6 dashes **Angostura bitters**

Muddle half the orange slices and syrup in the bottom of each highball glass. Fill the glasses with crushed ice and pour in the gin.

Stir, top with grapefruit juice and bitters and decorate with orange wedges. Serve with straws.

For The Fix, an even fruitier gin cocktail, mix 4 measures of gin with a dash each of lime, lemon and pineapple juice and 1 measure of Cointreau in a cocktail shaker full of ice. Strain into 2 chilled glasses.

berry collins

makes **2**

glasses **2 highball glasses**

equipment **muddling stick**

8 **raspberries**, plus extra to
  decorate
8 **blueberries**, plus extra to
  decorate
1–2 dashes **strawberry syrup**
crushed ice
4 measures **gin**
4 teaspoons **lemon juice**
sugar syrup, to taste
soda water, to top up
lemon slices, to decorate

Muddle half the berries and strawberry syrup in the bottom of each highball glass, then fill each glass with crushed ice.

Add the gin, lemon juice and sugar syrup. Stir well, then top up with soda water. Decorate with raspberries, blueberries and a lemon slice.

For a Lemon Grass Collins, to serve 1, put 2 measures of lemon grass vodka in a highball glass full of crushed ice, then layer ½ measure of vanilla liqueur, a dash of lemon juice, some sugar syrup and top up with ginger beer.

singapore sling

makes **2**

glasses **2 highball glasses**

equipment **cocktail shaker,
strainer, cocktail sticks**

ice cubes
2 measures **gin**
1 measure **cherry brandy**
½ measure **Cointreau**
½ measure **Benedictine**
1 measure **grenadine**
1 measure **lime juice**
10 measures **pineapple juice**
1 2 dashes **Angostura
bitters**

To decorate
pineapple wedges
maraschino cherries

Half-fill a cocktail shaker with ice cubes and put some ice cubes into each highball glass. Add the remaining ingredients to the shaker and shake until a frost forms on the outside of the shaker.

Strain over the ice into the glasses. Decorate each one with a pineapple wedge and a maraschino cherry and serve.

For a Gin Sling, shake the juice of 1 lemon, 2 measures of cherry brandy and 6 measures of gin with plenty of ice. Strain into 2 highball glasses filled with ice and top up with soda water.

bourbon peach smash

makes **2**

glasses **2 old-fashioned glasses**

equipment **muddling stick, cocktail shaker, strainer**

12 **mint leaves**, plus sprigs to decorate

6 **peach slices**

6 **lemon slices**, plus twists to decorate

4 teaspoons **caster sugar**

4 measures **bourbon**

ice cubes, plus crushed ice to serve

Muddle the mint leaves, peach and lemon slices and sugar in a cocktail shaker.

Add the bourbon and some ice cubes and shake well. Strain over cracked ice into 2 old-fashioned glasses. Decorate each with a mint sprig and a lemon slice.

For a Rhett Butler, another fruity bourbon concoction, half-fill a shaker with ice, then add 4 measures of bourbon, 8 measures of cranberry juice, 4 tablespoons of sugar syrup and 2 tablespoons of lime juice and shake well. Strain into 2 old-fashioned glasses filled with ice.

offshore

makes **2**

glasses **2 hurricane glasses**

equipment **food processor**

2 measures **white rum**

2 measures **tequila gold**

12 **mint leaves**, plus extra to
  decorate

4 **pineapple chunks**

6 measures **pineapple juice**

2 measures **single cream**

crushed ice

Put the rum, tequila, mint leaves, pineapple chunks, pineapple juice and single cream in a food processor or blender with some crushed ice and blend until the mixture is slushy.

Transfer to 2 hurricane glasses, decorate with mint leaves and serve.

For an Acapulco, another cocktail combining rum and tequila, put 2 measures each of ordinary tequila and white rum in an ice-filled shaker with 4 measures of pineapple juice, 2 measures of grapefruit juice and 2 measures of coconut syrup. Shake well, then strain into 2 highball glasses filled with ice.

playa del mar

makes **2**
glasses **2 highball glasses**
equipment **cocktail shaker,
  strainer**

2 **orange slices**
**light brown sugar and sea
  salt**, mixed
ice cubes
2½ measures **tequila gold**
1½ measures **Grand Marnier**
4 teaspoons **lime juice**
1½ measures **cranberry juice**
1½ measures **pineapple juice**
pineapple wedges,
  to decorate
orange rind spirals,
  to decorate

Frost the rim of each glass by moistening it with an orange slice, then pressing it into the sugar and salt mixture.

Fill each glass with ice cubes. Pour the tequila, Grand Marnier and fruit juices into a cocktail shaker. Fill the shaker with ice cubes and shake vigorously for 10 seconds, then strain into the glasses. Decorate each glass with a pineapple wedge and an orange rind spiral.

For a Sunburn, another tequila gold cocktail, to serve 1, fill a highball glass with ice, add 2 measures of tequila gold, 1 tablespoon of Cointreau and 150 ml (¼ pint) of cranberry juice. Decorate with an orange slice, if you like.

south for the summer

makes **2**
glasses **2 highball glasses**
equipment **food processor**

4 teaspoons **grenadine**
4 measures **tequila**
6 measures **orange juice**
8 fresh **pineapple chunks**
crushed ice
pineapple leaves, to decorate
orange rind spirals, to
   decorate

Pour half the grenadine gently into each glass. Put the tequila, orange juice and pineapple chunks into a food processor or blender with some crushed ice and blend until slushy.

Pour the mixture over the grenadine. Decorate each glass with a pineapple leaf and an orange rind spiral and stir just before serving.

For a Tequila Sunrise, put 5–6 ice cubes in a cocktail shaker, add 3 measures of tequila and 200 ml (7 fl oz) of fresh orange juice and shake to mix. Strain into 2 highball glasses over plenty of ice, then slowly pour 2 teaspoons of grenadine into each one, allowing it to settle. Decorate each glass with an orange slice.

brandy crusta

makes **2**

glasses **2 chilled martini glasses**

equipment **cocktail shaker, strainer**

lemon wedges
caster sugar
4 measures **brandy**
1 measure **orange Curaçao**
1 measure **maraschino liqueur**
2 measures **lemon juice**
6 dashes **Angostura bitters**
ice cubes
lemon rind strips, to decorate

Moisten the rim of each glass with a lemon wedge, then dip it in the caster sugar.

Put the brandy, Curaçao, maraschino, lemon juice and bitters into a cocktail shaker with some ice cubes and shake well. Strain into the glasses, decorate each with lemon rind strips and serve.

For a Rum Crusta, use dark rum and zesty Cointreau instead of the brandy and Curaçao, use lime juice instead of lemon juice and omit the bitters.

Monte Carlo sling

makes **2**

glasses **2 highball glasses**

equipment **muddling stick, cocktail shaker, strainer, cocktail sticks**

10 **seedless grapes**, plus extra to decorate

crushed ice

2 measures **brandy**

1 measure **peach liqueur**

2 measures **ruby port**

2 measures **lemon juice**

1 measure **orange juice**

2 dashes **orange bitters**

4 measures **Champagne**

Muddle 5 grapes in the base of each highball glass, then fill the glass with crushed ice.

Put all the other ingredients, except the Champagne, into a cocktail shaker and add more ice. Shake well and strain into the glasses. Top up with the Champagne, decorate with grapes and serve.

For a Fuzzy Navel, to serve 1, one of the easiest cocktails to prepare, simply pour 1½ measures of peach liqueur into a highball glass. Add plenty of ice and top up with fresh orange juice.

goombay smash

makes **2**

glasses **2 old-fashioned glasses**

equipment **cocktail shaker, strainer, cocktail sticks**

3 measures **coconut rum**
2 measures **cachaça**
1 measure **apricot brandy**
1 measure **lime juice**
8 measures **pineapple juice**
ice cubes

To decorate
pineapple wedges
lime twists
maraschino cherries

Put the rum, cachaça, brandy, lime juice and pineapple juice in a cocktail shaker and add some ice cubes.

Shake and strain over more ice into 2 old-fashioned glasses. Decorate each glass with a pineapple slice, a lime twist and some cherries and serve.

To make a Banana Royal, which has the same essential ingredients, to serve 1, blend some crushed ice with 1½ measures each of coconut milk and golden rum, 3 measures of pineapple juice, ½ measure of double cream and a banana. Process until smooth and creamy then serve in a highball glass and sprinkle with desiccated coconut.

cool and refreshing

mexican mule

makes **2**
glasses **2 highball glasses**
equipment **muddling stick**

2 **limes**
2 dashes **sugar syrup**
crushed ice
2 measures **José Cuervo Gold tequila**
2 measures **Kahlúa coffee liqueur**
ginger ale, to top up

Cut the limes into wedges. Put half in each highball glass and muddle with the sugar syrup.

Half-fill each glass with crushed ice, add the tequila and Kahlúa, stir and top up with ginger ale.

For a Moscow Mule, an American favourite from the 1950s, put 6–8 cracked ice cubes in a cocktail shaker, add 4 measures of vodka and the freshly squeezed juice of 4 limes and shake well. Pour, without straining, into 2 highball glasses over ice and top up with ginger beer.

horizon

makes **2**

glasses **2 chilled martini glasses**

equipment **cocktail shaker, strainer**

3 measures **Zubrowka Bison Grass vodka**

1 measure **Xante pear liqueur**

2 measures **pressed apple juice**

2 teaspoons **passion fruit liqueur**

2 dashes **lemon juice**

ice cubes

lemon twists, to decorate (optional)

Pour all the ingredients into a cocktail shaker with some ice cubes.

Shake and double-strain into chilled martini glasses, decorate each with a lemon twist, if you like, and serve.

For a Cosmopolitan, another fruity vodka combination, shake together 2 measures of vodka, 1 measure of Cointreau, 2 measures of cranberry juice, the juice of 1 lime and some cracked ice. Strain into 2 chilled martini glasses and decorate with orange twists.

fragrance

makes **2**

glasses **2 highball glasses**

equipment **cocktail shaker, strainer, straws**

ice cubes, plus crushed ice to serve

3 measures **vodka**

1 measure **Midori**

2 measures **lemon juice**

2 measures **pineapple juice**

2 dashes **sugar syrup**

2 **lemon wedges**

Put 8–12 ice cubes with the vodka, Midori, fruit juices and sugar syrup into a cocktail shaker and shake.

Strain into 2 highball glasses filled with crushed ice. Squeeze a lemon wedge over each drink, drop it in and serve with straws.

For a Machete, which is not quite so sweet, shake 2 measures of vodka with 4 measures of pineapple juice and plenty of ice. Strain over ice into 2 highball glasses and top up with tonic water.

hair raiser

makes **2**

glasses **2 highball glasses**

equipment **straws**

cracked ice cubes

2 measures **vodka**

2 measures **sweet vermouth**

2 measures **tonic water**

lemon and lime rind spirals,
   to decorate

Put 2–4 cracked ice cubes into 2 highball glasses and pour over the vodka, vermouth and tonic water.

Stir lightly, decorate with the lemon and lime rind spirals and serve with straws.

For a Le Mans, another refreshing drink, replace the vermouth with Cointreau and the tonic water with soda water. Decorate with lemon wedges.

mojito

makes **2**

glasses **2 highball glasses**

equipment **muddling stick**

16 **mint leaves**, plus sprigs
    to decorate

1 **lime,** cut into wedges

4 teaspoons **cane sugar**

crushed ice

5 measures **white rum**

soda water, to top up

Muddle the mint leaves, lime and sugar in the bottom
of 2 highball glasses and fill with crushed ice.

Add the rum, stir and top up with soda water.
Decorate with mint sprigs and serve.

For a Limon Mojito, a citrus version of the classic
Mojito, muddle the quarters of 2 limes with
4 teaspoons of soft brown sugar and 16 mint leaves
in the bottom of 2 highball glasses, then add
4 measures of Limon Bacardi rum instead of the
5 measures of white rum. Stir and top up with soda
water, if you like. Decorate with lemon and lime slices
and drink through straws.

cuba libre

makes **2**
glasses **2 highball glasses**
equipment **straws**

ice cubes
4 measures **golden rum**, such
    as Havana Club 3-year-old
juice of 1 lime
cola, to top up
lime wedges

Fill 2 highball glasses with ice cubes. Pour over the rum and lime juice and stir.

Top up with cola, decorate with lime wedges and serve with straws.

For a First the Money, a minty alternative to a Cuba Libre, muddle 8 lime wedges with 2 dashes of crème de menthe. Add some crushed ice, 2 measures of dark rum and 2 measures of coffee liqueur. Serve over ice in 2 old-fashioned glasses and top up with cola.

tom collins

makes **2**
glasses **2 highball glasses**

4 measures **gin**
3 teaspoons **lemon juice**
2 teaspoons **sugar syrup**
ice cubes
soda water, to top up
lemon slices, to decorate

Put the gin, lemon juice and sugar syrup into 2 highball glasses.

Stir well and fill the glasses with ice cubes. Top up with soda water, add a lemon slice to each glass and serve.

For a Pedro Collins, replace the gin with rum, and for a Pierre Collins, use brandy instead.

negroni

makes **2**

glasses **2 old-fashioned glasses**

equipment **mixing glass, strainer**

ice cubes

2 measures **Plymouth gin**

2 measures **Campari**

2 measures **red vermouth**

soda water, to top up (optional)

orange wedges, to decorate

Put some ice cubes into a mixing glass and fill 2 old-fashioned glasses with ice cubes.

Add the gin, Campari and vermouth to the mixing glass, stir briefly to mix and strain over the ice in the glasses. Top up with soda water, if liked. Decorate each glass with some orange wedges and serve.

For a Bronx, a more citrussy version, use 2 measures of sweet vermouth instead of the Campari and 2 measures of dry vermouth instead of the red vermouth. Serve in 2 chilled martini glasses and top up with fresh orange juice.

white lady

makes **2**

glasses **2 chilled martini glasses**

equipment **cocktail shaker, strainer**

2 measures **gin**

2 measures **Cointreau**

2 measures **lemon juice**

lemon twists

Pour the gin, Cointreau and lemon juice into a cocktail shaker.

Shake and strain into 2 chilled martini glasses, add a twist of lemon to each and serve.

For a Lady of Leisure, which is a pretty pink cocktail, use 2 measures of gin, 1 measure of Chambord and 1 measure of Cointreau, a dash of lemon juice and 50 ml (2 fl oz) of pineapple juice. Shake and strain into 2 chilled martini glasses and decorate with strips of orange rind.

classic martini

makes **2**

glasses **2 chilled martini glasses**

equipment **mixing glass, strainer, cocktail sticks**

ice cubes

1 measure **dry vermouth**

6 measures **gin**

stuffed green olives, to decorate

Put 10–12 ice cubes into a mixing glass.

Pour over the vermouth and gin and stir (never shake) vigorously and evenly without splashing. Strain into 2 chilled martini glasses, decorate each with a green olive and serve.

For a Smoky Martini, an interesting twist on the classic martini, to serve 1, put some ice cubes into a mixing glass, add ¼ measure dry vermouth and stir until the ice cubes are well coated. Pour in 2 measures of gin and 1 measure of sloe gin then add 5 drops of orange bitters. Stir well, then strain into a chilled cocktail glass and add an orange twist.

virginia mint julep

makes **2**
glasses **2 highball glasses**
equipment **muddling stick**

18 **mint sprigs**, plus extra
   to decorate
2 teaspoons **sugar syrup**
crushed ice
6 measures **bourbon**

Muddle half the mint and sugar syrup in the bottom of each glass (or, traditionally, iced silver mugs).

Fill the glasses with crushed ice. Pour the bourbon over the ice and stir gently. Pack in more crushed ice and stir until a frost forms on the outside of the glasses. Wrap each glass in a table napkin and serve decorated with a mint sprig.

For a Mint Julep, which dates from 1803, use 4 measures of bourbon instead of 6 and add 8 dashes of Angostura bitters to the muddled mixture, then pour into 2 highball glasses.

tijuana sling

makes **2**

glasses **2 highball glasses**

equipment **cocktail shaker**

3½ measures **tequila**

1½ measures **crème de cassis**

1½ measures **lime juice**

4 dashes **Peychaud's bitters**

ice cubes

7 measures **ginger ale**

To decorate

lime slices

blueberries

Pour the tequila, crème de cassis, lime juice and bitters into a cocktail shaker. Add 8–10 ice cubes and shake vigorously.

Pour into 2 highball glasses without straining and top up with the ginger ale. Decorate with lime slices and blueberries and serve.

For a Border Crossing, which makes a good summer drink, use tequila gold instead of tequila, 2 measures of lime juice, 1 teaspoon honey and a several dashes of orange bitters. Top up the 2 highball glasses with ginger ale and decorate with blueberries and lime wedges.

long island iced tea

makes **2**

glasses **2 highball glasses**

equipment **cocktail shaker, strainer**

1 measure **vodka**
1 measure **gin**
1 measure **white rum**
1 measure **tequila**
1 measure **Cointreau**
1 measure **lemon juice**
ice cubes
cola, to top up
lemon slices, to decorate

Put the vodka, gin, rum, tequila, Cointreau and lemon juice in a cocktail shaker with some ice cubes and shake to mix.

Strain into 2 highball glasses filled with ice cubes and top up with cola. Decorate with lemon slices and serve.

For a Camber Sands Iced Tea, the British equivalent of the potent Long Island Iced Tea, shake 4 measures of lemon vodka with 200 ml (7 fl oz) of Earl Grey tea, 50 ml (2 fl oz) of cranberry juice and 12 mint leaves, a dash of sugar syrup, some lemon juice and plenty of ice. Strain over ice into 2 highball glasses and decorate with lemon slices and mint leaves.

bedtime bouncer

makes **2**
glasses **2 highball glasses**
equipment **mixing glass,
  straws**

4 measures **brandy**
2 measures **Cointreau**
10 measures **bitter lemon**
ice cubes
lemon rind spirals,
  to decorate

Pour the brandy, Cointreau and bitter lemon into a mixing glass and stir well.

Put 8–12 ice cubes in 2 highball glasses and pour the mixture over the ice. Decorate with lemon rind spirals and serve with straws.

For a Bouncing Bomb, use Curaçao instead of Cointreau and top up with soda water rather than bitter lemon.

sangria

serves **10–12**
glasses **wine glasses**
equipment **very large jug**

ice cubes
2 bottles light Spanish **red
wine**, chilled
5 measures **brandy**
**orange, lemon and apple
wedges**
lemon slices
cinnamon sticks
about 450 ml (¾ pint) **chilled
lemonade**, to top up

Put some ice cubes into a very large jug. Add the wine, brandy, fruit wedges and one cinnamon stick and stir well.

Top up with lemonade when you are ready to serve, and stir. Serve in glasses decorated with lemon slices and cinnamon sticks.

For a White Sangria, use white wine instead of red. To serve 6 people, pour 2 large glasses of dry white wine into a jug, add 2 measures of lemon vodka, 2 of peach schnapps, 2 of peach purée, 1 of lemon juice and 1 of lime juice. Chill for 12 hours or overnight in the refrigerator. Just before serving, add ice cubes and 1 measure each of freshly squeezed lemon and lime juice and top up with lemonade.

pimm's cocktail

makes **2**
glasses **2 highball glasses**
equipment **muddling stick**

ice cubes
2 measures **Pimm's No. 1**
2 measures **gin**
4 measures **lemonade**
4 measures **ginger ale**

To decorate
cucumber strips
blueberries
orange slices

Fill 2 highball glass with ice cubes.

Add the remaining ingredients, one by one in order, over the ice. Decorate with cucumber strips, blueberries and orange slices and serve.

For On the Lawn, which is more powerful than the classic Pimm's Cocktail but just as refreshing, fill 2 highball glasses with ice and fresh fruit, add 2 measures of Pimm's No. 1 and 2 measures of gin to each one and top up with lemonade and ginger ale.

planter's punch

makes **2**
glasses **2 highball glasses**
equipment **cocktail shaker,
    strainer**

4 measures **Myer's Jamaican
    Planter's Punch rum**
8 drops **Angostura bitters**
1 measure **lime juice**
4 measures **chilled water**
2 measures **sugar syrup**
ice cubes

To decorate
orange slices
lime slices

Put the rum, bitters, lime juice, water and sugar syrup
into a cocktail shaker and add some ice cubes.

Shake and strain into 2 ice-filled highball glasses.
Decorate with slices of orange and lime and serve.

For a Tempo, a quick alternative to a planter's punch,
put 3 cracked ice cubes into each glass and pour
1 measure each of white rum and lime juice and
1/2 measure of crème de cacao into each one. Add a
dash of Angostura bitters, stir, top up with lemonade
and decorate with slices of lime.

sparkling gems

russian spring punch

makes **2**
glasses **2 highball glasses**

ice cubes
1 measure **crème de cassis**
2 measures **lemon juice**
4 tablespoons **sugar syrup**
chilled Champagne, to top
  up
4 measures **Absolut vodka**

To decorate
lemon slices
mixed berries

Fill 2 highball glasses with ice cubes. Pour over the crème de cassis, lemon juice and sugar syrup.

Add the Champagne and vodka at the same time (this prevents excessive fizzing) and stir. Decorate each glass with a lemon slice and some berries and serve.

For a Kir Champagne Royale, which is not as strong as the Russian Spring Punch, to serve 1, put 1 teaspoon of vodka into a Champagne flute, add 2 teaspoons of crème de cassis and top up with chilled Champagne.

lime fizz

makes **2**

glasses **2 chilled Champagne flutes**

equipment **cocktail shaker, strainer**

2 **lime wedges**

2 measures **lime vodka**

2 measures **orange juice**

ice cubes

chilled Champagne, to top up

lime rind twists, to decorate

Squeeze the lime wedges into a cocktail shaker and add the vodka and orange juice with some ice cubes.

Shake briefly and double-strain into 2 chilled Champagne flutes. Top up with chilled Champagne and decorate with lime rind twists.

For a Grand Mimosa, another fruity and refreshing sparkler, to serve 1, pour 1 measure of Grand Marnier and 1 measure fresh orange juice into a Champagne flute, add some ice and top up with chilled Champagne.

buck's twizz

makes **2**

glasses **2 chilled Champagne
saucers**

2 measures **chilled orange
juice**
1 measure **maraschino
liqueur**
2 measures **Absolut
Mandarin vodka**
chilled Champagne, to top up
**rindless pink grapefruit
slices**, to decorate

Pour the orange juice and maraschino into 2 chilled
Champagne saucers.

Add the vodka and Champagne at the same time
(this prevents excessive fizzing). Decorate with rindless
pink grapefruit slices and serve.

For a Buck's Fizz, that much-loved party drink, you
need a mixture of orange juice and Champagne. Use
about 250 ml (8 fl oz) of fresh orange juice to a bottle
of chilled Champagne and mix them in a large jug.

lush crush

makes **2**

glasses **2 chilled Champagne flutes**

equipment **muddling stick, cocktail shaker, strainer**

4 **strawberries**, plus extra to decorate

2 dashes **sugar syrup**

4 **lime wedges**

2 measures **Absolut Kurant vodka**

ice cubes

chilled Champagne, to top up

Muddle the strawberries, sugar syrup and lime wedges in the bottom of a cocktail shaker. Add the vodka and some ice cubes.

Shake and double-strain into 2 chilled Champagne flutes. Top up with chilled Champagne, decorate each glass with a sliced strawberry and serve.

For a Champino, which is equally sparkling but rather less fruity than the Lush Crush, shake 2 measures of Campari with 2½ measures of sweet vermouth and plenty of ice, then strain into chilled martini glasses. Top up with chilled Champagne. This cocktail has a pleasant, bittersweet aftertaste.

riviera fizz

makes **2**

glasses **2 chilled Champagne flutes**

equipment **cocktail shaker, strainer**

3 measures **sloe gin**
1 measure **lemon juice**
1 measure **sugar syrup**
ice cubes
chilled Champagne, to top up
lemon twists, to decorate

Put the sloe gin, lemon juice and sugar syrup into a cocktail shaker and add some ice cubes.

Shake and strain into 2 chilled Champagne flutes. Top up with chilled Champagne, stir and decorate each glass with a lemon twist.

For a Classic Champagne Cocktail, the ultimate sparkling drink, place a sugar cube in each Champagne flute, saturate it with Angostura bitters then add 1 measure of brandy. Top up with chilled Champagne.

e = mc²

makes **2**
glasses **2 Champagne flutes**
equipment **cocktail shaker,
strainer**

crushed ice cubes
4 measures **Southern
Comfort**
2 measures **lemon juice**
1 measure **maple syrup**
chilled Champagne, to top up
lemon rind strips, to decorate

Put 8–10 crushed ice cubes into a cocktail shaker.
Pour the Southern Comfort, lemon juice and maple
syrup over the ice and shake until a frost forms on
the outside of the shaker.

Strain into 2 Champagne flutes and top up with
chilled Champagne. Decorate with a lemon rind strip
and serve.

For Paddy's Night, a sparkling green cocktail, pour
1 measure each of crème de menthe and Irish
whiskey into a cocktail shaker with some ice cubes.
Shake, strain into 2 Champagne flutes and top up
with chilled Champagne.

champagne julep

makes **2**

glasses **2 highball glasses**

equipment **muddling stick**

4 **mint sprigs**, plus extra
  to decorate

2 tablespoons **sugar syrup**

crushed ice

2 measures **brandy**

chilled Champagne, to top up

Put 2 mint sprigs and 1 tablespoon sugar syrup into each glass and muddle together.

Fill the glasses with crushed ice, then add the brandy. Top up with chilled Champagne and stir gently. Decorate with mint sprigs and serve.

For a Champagne Cooler, which couldn't be simpler, replace the sugar syrup with 1 measure of Cointreau.

bellini

makes **2**

glasses **2 Champagne flutes**

equipment **mixing glass**

4 measures **peach juice**

8 measures **chilled
Champagne**

2 dashes **grenadine** (optional)

peach wedges, to decorate

Mix together the peach juice and chilled Champagne
in a large mixing glass. Add the grenadine (if used).

Pour into 2 Champagne flutes, decorate each glass
with a peach wedge and serve.

For a Mango Bellini, to serve 1, a fruity variation on
the theme, pour 3 measures of mango juice into a
Champagne flute and top up with chilled pink
Champagne.

aria classic

makes **2**
glasses **2 chilled Champagne flutes**

2 **brown sugar cubes**
6 drops **Angostura bitters**
2 measures **Grand Marnier**
chilled Champagne, to top up
orange twists, to decorate

Put a sugar cube in the bottom of each glass and add 3 drops of bitters to each.

Add the Grand Marnier and stir briefly. Top up with chilled Champagne, decorate each glass with an orange twist and serve.

For a Frobisher, which is stronger stuff, fill highball glasses with ice, add a couple of shakes of Angostura bitters and 1 measure of gin to each one and top up with chilled Champagne.

ritz fizz 1

makes **2**
glasses **2 Champagne flutes**
equipment **mixing glass**

2 dashes **blue Curaçao**
2 dashes **lemon juice**
2 dashes **Amaretto di
  Saronno**
chilled Champagne, to top up
lemon rind spirals,
  to decorate

Pour the Curaçao, lemon juice and Amaretto into a mixing glass and mix together.

Transfer to Champagne flutes and top up with chilled Champagne. Stir gently to mix, decorate each glass with a lemon rind spiral and serve.

For a Ritz Fizz 2, mix equal measures of crème de cassis, Poire William and chilled Champagne and serve in chilled Champagne flutes. This is easy to drink but deceptively strong.

tangy tongue teasers

surf rider

makes **2**
glasses **2 old-fashioned
  glasses**
equipment **cocktail shaker,
  strainer**

ice cubes
6 measures **vodka**
2 measures **sweet vermouth**
juice of **1 lemon**
juice of **2 oranges**
1 teaspoon **grenadine**

Put 8–10 ice cubes into a cocktail shaker. Pour the vodka, vermouth, fruit juices and grenadine over the ice and shake until a frost forms on the ouside of the shaker.

Strain and pour into old-fashioned glasses. Serve immediately.

For a Tokyo Jo, which has a melon rather than a citrus flavour, put 2 measures of vodka and 2 measures of Midori into a cocktail shaker with some ice. Shake well and serve over ice in 2 old-fashioned glasses.

godmother

makes **2**

glasses **2 old-fashioned glasses**

cracked ice cubes
3 measures **vodka**
1 measure **Amaretto di Saronno**

Put 4–6 cracked ice cubes into 2 old-fashioned glasses.

Add the vodka and Amaretto, stir lightly to mix and serve.

For a St Petersburg, replace the Amaretto with the same amount of Chartreuse.

vodka sazerac

makes **2**
glasses **2 old-fashioned glasses**

2 **sugar cubes**
4 drops **Angostura bitters**
5 drops **Pernod**
6–8 **ice cubes**
4 measures **vodka**
lemonade, to top up

Put a sugar cube in each old-fashioned glass and shake 2 drops of bitters over each.

Add the Pernod and swirl it around to coat the inside of each glass. Drop in 3–4 ice cubes and pour in the vodka. Top up with lemonade, stir gently to mix and serve.

For an Iceberg, a cloudy pastis with a mighty punch, omit the lemonade and Angostura bitters and serve over ice in old-fashioned glasses.

dawa

makes **2**

glasses **2 old-fashioned glasses**

equipment **muddling stick**

2 **limes**, quartered and thickly sliced

2 tablespoons **thick honey**

2 teaspoons **caster sugar**

crushed ice

4 measures **vodka**

Put the lime slices, honey and sugar in 2 heavy-based old-fashioned glasses and muddle together.

Add some crushed ice and pour over the vodka.

For a Strawberry Dawa, an African favourite, muddle 6 strawberries and 2 sliced limes in old-fashioned glasses. Add a splash of strawberry syrup, some ice and 2 measures of lemon vodka to each one.

vanilla vodka sour

makes **2**

glasses **2 martini glasses**

equipment **cocktail shaker**

ice cubes

4 measures **vanilla vodka**

1 measure **sugar syrup**

2 **egg whites**

3 measures **lemon juice**

10 drops **Angostura bitters**, to decorate

Put 8–10 ice cubes into a cocktail shaker. Add the vodka, sugar syrup, egg whites and lemon juice and shake until a frost forms on the outside of the shaker.

Pour, without straining, into 2 martini glasses and shake the Angostura bitters on top to decorate.

For a Vodka Collins, shake together 6 ice cubes, 4 measures of vodka, the juice of 2 fresh limes and 2 teaspoons caster sugar. Strain into 2 highball glasses, add fresh ice cubes and top up with soda water.

gingersnap

makes **2**

glasses **2 old-fashioned glasses**

ice cubes
6 measures **vodka**
2 measures **ginger wine**
soda water, to top up

Put 4–6 ice cubes into 2 old-fashioned glasses.

Pour over the vodka and ginger wine and stir lightly. Top up with soda water and serve.

For a Salty Dog, which has a citrus note, dip 2 old-fashioned glasses in salt then put 2–3 ice cubes into each one. Add 1 measure of vodka to each glass and top up with grapefruit juice.

margarita

makes **2**

glasses **2 margarita glasses**

equipment **cocktail shaker,
strainer**

2 **lime wedges**

rock salt

4 measures **Herrudura
Reposado tequila**

2 measures **lime juice**

2 measures **Triple Sec**

ice cubes

lime slices, to decorate

Rub the rim of each margarita (coupette) glass with a lime wedge, then dip it into rock salt.

Pour the tequila, lime juice and Triple Sec into a cocktail shaker and add some ice cubes. Shake and strain into the salt-rimmed glasses. Decorate each glass with a slice of lime and serve.

For a Grand Margarita, replace the Triple Sec with Grand Marnier. This brings a sweet twist to the classic Margarita.

hummingbird

makes **2**
glasses **2 highball glasses**
equipment **cocktail shaker,
strainer, straws**

crushed ice cubes
2 measures **dark rum**
2 measures **light rum**
2 measures **Southern
Comfort**
2 measures **orange juice**
cola, to top up
orange slices, to decorate

Put 8–10 crushed ice cubes into a cocktail shaker.
Pour the rums, Southern Comfort and orange juice over
the ice and shake until a frost forms on the outside of
the shaker.

Strain into 2 highball glasses and top up with cola.
Decorate each glass with an orange slice and serve
with a straw.

For a Havana Beach, another cocktail with Cuban
connections, put 2 measures of white rum, 1 peeled
lime, 4 measures of pineapple juice and 2 teaspoons
of sugar into a blender. Whiz until smooth, then tip
into 2 highball glasses over plenty of ice and top up
with ginger ale.

rum old-fashioned

makes **2**

glasses **2 old-fashioned glasses**

6 **ice cubes**
2 dashes **Angostura bitters**
2 dashes **lime bitters**
2 teaspoons **caster sugar**
1 measure **water**
4 measures **white rum**
1 measure **dark rum**
lime rind twists, to decorate

Stir 1 ice cube with a dash of both bitters, 1 teaspoon sugar and half the water in each old-fashioned glass until the sugar has dissolved.

Add the white rum, stir and add the remaining ice cubes. Add the dark rum and stir again. Decorate each glass with a lime rind twist and serve.

For a Rum Refashioned, put a brown sugar cube in each old-fashioned glass, splash it with some Angostura bitters, then add 2 ice cubes and 2 measures of aged rum to each glass, stir well then add sugar syrup to taste.

tanqstream

makes **2**
glasses **2 highball glasses**
equipment **cocktail shaker, strainer**

cracked ice cubes
4 measures **Tanqueray gin**
4 teaspoons **lime juice**
6 measures **soda water or tonic water**
4 teaspoons **crème de cassis**

To decorate
lime slices
mixed berries

Put some cracked ice with the gin and lime juice into a cocktail shaker and shake to mix.

Strain into 2 highball glasses, each half-filled with cracked ice. For a dry Tanqstream, add soda water; for a less dry drink, add tonic water. Stir in the crème de cassis, decorate with the lime slices and mixed berries and serve.

For a Gin and Tonic at its best, to serve 1, pour 2 measures of gin and 4 measures of tonic into an old-fashioned glass with plenty of ice cubes and a wedge of lime.

pink clover club

makes **2**
glasses **2 martini glasses**
equipment **cocktail shaker,
  strainer**

ice cubes
juice of 2 **limes**
2 dashes **grenadine**
2 **egg whites**
6 measures **gin**
strawberry slices, to decorate

Put 8–10 ice cubes into a cocktail shaker and pour the lime juice, grenadine, egg whites and gin over the ice. Shake until a frost forms on the outside of the shaker.

Strain into 2 martini glasses and decorate each glass with strawberry slices.

For a Clover Club, a classic that dates from the 1880s, omit the grenadine and add a splash of sugar syrup. Strain into 2 glasses and decorate with lime wedges.

sapphire martini

makes **2**
glasses **2 martini glasses**
equipment **cocktail shaker,
  strainer**

ice cubes
4 measures **gin**
1 measure **blue Curaçao**
red or blue cocktail cherries,
  to decorate

Put 8 ice cubes into a cocktail shaker. Pour in the gin and blue Curaçao. Shake well to mix.

Strain into 2 martini glasses and carefully drop a cherry into each glass.

For a Gimlet, another simple gin-based cocktail, to serve 1, mix 2 measures of gin and 1 measure of lime cordial in an old-fashioned glass, and add plenty of ice. Decorate with a wedge of lime.

rattlesnake

makes **2**

glasses **2 old-fashioned glasses**

equipment **cocktail shaker, strainer**

ice cubes, plus extra to serve
3 measures **whisky**
2 teaspoons **lemon juice**
2 teaspoons **sugar syrup**
2 **egg whites**
few drops **Pernod**
lime wedges, to decorate

Put 8–10 ice cubes, the whisky, lemon juice, sugar syrup, egg whites and Pernod into a cocktail shaker and shake extremely well.

Strain into 2 old-fashioned glasses, add some more ice and serve with lime wedges.

For a Kicker, which is one of the simplest whisky-based cocktails, to serve 1, mix 1 measure of whisky with 1 measure of Midori and serve chilled or with ice.

american belle

makes **2**
glasses **2 shot glasses**
equipment **bar spoon**

1 measure **cherry liqueur**
1 measure **Amaretto di Saronno**
1 measure **bourbon**

Pour the cherry liqueur into 2 shot glasses. Using the back of a bar spoon, slowly float the Amaretto over the cherry liqueur to form a separate layer.

Layer the bourbon over the Amaretto in the same way and serve.

For a Sicilian Kiss, another Amaretto cocktail, to serve 1, fill an old-fashioned glass with crushed ice, pour in 2 measures of Southern Comfort and 1 measure of Amaretto di Saronno and stir.

baja sour

makes **2**
glasses **2 highball glasses**
equipment **cocktail shaker**

ice cubes
2½ measures **tequila gold**
4 teaspoons **sugar syrup**
2½ measures **lemon juice**
4 dashes **orange bitters**
1 **egg white**
2 tablespoons **Amontillado sherry**
lemon wedges, to decorate
orange rind spirals,
   to decorate

Put 8–10 ice cubes into a cocktail shaker with the tequila, sugar syrup, lemon juice, bitters and egg white and shake vigorously.

Pour into 2 highball glasses and drizzle over the sherry. Decorate each glass with lemon wedges and an orange rind spiral and serve.

For a Batanga, another tequila cocktail, dip a lime wedge in some salt and rub it around the rim of 2 highball glasses. Fill the glasses with ice, add 2 measures of tequila to each and top up with cola.

dirty sanchez

makes **2**

glasses **2 chilled martini glasses**

equipment **mixing glass, strainer, cocktail sticks**

ice cubes

4 teaspoons **Noilly Prat**

4 measures **tequila gold** (preferably Anejo)

4 teaspoons **brine from a jar of black olives**

4 **black olives**, to decorate

Fill a mixing glass with ice cubes and add the Noilly Prat. Stir to coat the ice thoroughly, then pour away the excess vermouth.

Add the tequila and brine and stir until thoroughly chilled. Strain into 2 chilled martini glasses, decorate with black olives and serve.

For a Pancho Villa, shake 2 measures of tequila with 1 measure of Tia Maria, 2 teaspoons of Cointreau and lots of ice, then strain into chilled martini glasses.

pisco sour

makes **2**

glasses **2 old-fashioned glasses**

equipment **cocktail shaker, strainer**

ice cubes

4 measures **Pisco**

2 measures **lemon juice**

4 teaspoons **caster sugar**

2 **egg whites**

2 dashes **Angostura bitters**

lemon wedges, to decorate

Half-fill a cocktail shaker with ice cubes and fill 2 old-fashioned glasses with ice cubes.

Add the Pisco, lemon juice, sugar and egg whites to the shaker and shake until a frost forms on the outside of the shaker.

Strain over the ice in the glasses, add the bitters to the frothy head and serve with lemon wedges.

For the Atacama Pisco Sour, the Chilean version of the Pisco Sour, omit the egg whites and Angostura bitters, use a little less Pisco and add ½ measure of Scotch whisky to each glass.

batida maracuja

makes **2**
glasses **2 highball glasses**
equipment **cocktail shaker,
  straws**

4 measures **cachaça**
4 **passion fruit**, cut in half and
  the pulp squeezed out
2 measures **sugar syrup**
2 measures **lemon juice**
ice cubes, plus crushed ice
  to serve
lemon slices, to decorate

Put the cachaça, passion fruit pulp, sugar syrup
and lemon juice into a cocktail shaker and add
some ice cubes.

Shake and strain into 2 highball glasses filled with
crushed ice. Decorate with slices of lemon and serve
with long straws.

For a Caipirinha, the best-known Brazilian cocktail,
and another cachaça concoction, muddle 4 lime
wedges in each old-fashioned glass with a couple of
teaspoons of cane sugar. Top with crushed ice and
2 measures of cachaça.

cucumber sake-tini

makes **2**

glasses **2 chilled martini glasses**

equipment **mixing glass, strainer**

ice cubes

5 measures **cucumber-infused sake**

3 measures **gin**

1 measure **Curaçao**

cucumber slices, to decorate

Put some ice cubes in a mixing glass with the sake, gin and Curaçao and stir until thoroughly chilled.

Strain into 2 chilled martini glasses, decorate with cucumber slices and serve.

For a Sake-tini, pour 5 measures of sake into a mixing glass with 2 measures of vodka and 1 measure of orange Curaçao. Mix well, then pour into 2 chilled martini glasses.

winter
warmers

rusty nail

makes **2**
glasses **2 old-fashioned glasses**

ice cubes
3 measures **Scotch whisky**
2 measures **Drambuie**

Fill 2 old-fashioned glasses with ice cubes.

Pour over the whisky and Drambuie and serve.

For a Whisky Mac, to serve 1, a great pick-me-up on a cold day, combine equal quantities of Scotch whisky and ginger wine. Serve with ice if you like.

Mexican marshmallow mocha

makes **2**
glasses **2 toddy glasses**

4 teaspoons **cocoa powder**,
  plus extra to decorate
2 measures **Kahlúa coffee
  liqueur**
7 measures **hot filter coffee**
mini marshmallows
whipped cream

Put 2 teaspoons cocoa powder into each toddy glass, add the Kahlúa and coffee and stir until mixed.

Drop in the mini marshmallows and float the cream on top. Decorate with cocoa powder and serve.

For an Irish Coffee, warm hot toddy glasses and add 1 teaspoon of sugar and 1 measure of Irish whiskey to each one. Fill the glasses two-thirds full with hot filter coffee and stir until the sugar has dissolved. Float lightly whipped double cream over the top, pouring it over the back of a cold spoon. Decorate with coffee granules, if liked.

early night

makes **2**
glasses **2 toddy glasses**

2 tablespoons **lemon juice**
2 measures **clear honey**
2 measures **whisky**
4 measures **boiling water**
2 measures **ginger wine**
lemon slices, to decorate

Put the lemon juice and honey into 2 toddy glasses and stir well. Add the whisky and continue stirring. Stir in the boiling water, then add the ginger wine.

Decorate each glass with lemon slices. Serve at once and drink while still hot.

For an Aberdeen Angus, to serve 1, warm 1 measure of Drambuie. Pour it into a ladle and ignite. When the flames have died down, add it to a mug containing 1 measure of Scotch whisky, 1 teaspoon of clear honey and 2 teaspoons of lime juice and stir well.

pudding cocktail

makes **2**

glasses **2 martini glasses**

equipment **cocktail shaker, strainer**

2 measures **Calvados**

3 measures **brandy**

2 **egg yolks**

2 teaspoons **caster sugar**

ice cubes

ground cinnamon, to decorate

Put the Calvados, brandy, egg yolks and caster sugar into a cocktail shaker with some ice cubes and shake until well mixed.

Strain into chilled martini glasses. Light a long taper, hold it over each glass in turn and sprinkle cinnamon through the flame on to the surface of the drink.

For an Apple Posset, an old-fashioned English country drink, warm 500 ml (17 fl oz) of apple juice in a saucepan. Meanwhile, put 1 teaspoon of brown sugar in each of 2 toddy glasses with 2 measures of Calvados. Divide the apple juice between the mugs, add a cinnamon stick to each one and stir.

glögg

serves **15–20**

glasses **small cups or heatproof wine glasses**

2 bottles **dry red wine**, or 1 bottle **red wine** and 1 bottle **port or Madeira**

rind of **1 orange**

20 **cardamom pods**, lightly crushed

2 **cinnamon sticks**

20 whole **cloves**

175 g (6 oz) **blanched almonds**

250 g (8 oz) **raisins**

250–375 g (8–12 oz) **sugar cubes**

300 ml (½ pint) **Aquavit or brandy**

Put the wine or wine and port or Madeira into a saucepan. Tie the orange rind and spices in a piece of muslin and add to the pan. Add the almonds and raisins. Heat at just below boiling point for 25 minutes, stirring occasionally.

Put a wire rack over the pan and put the sugar cubes on it. Warm the Aquavit or brandy and pour it over the sugar cubes to saturate them evenly. Set them alight: they will melt through the wire rack into the wine.

Stir the glögg and remove the spice bag. Serve hot, putting a few raisins and almonds in each cup.

For glühwein, to serve 6, spike a lemon with 8 cloves and place in a saucepan with 1 bottle of red wine, 125 g (4 oz) sugar and 2 cinnamon sticks. Simmer gently for 10 minutes, then lower the heat and add 150 ml (¼ pint) brandy. Strain and serve in mugs or heatproof glasses with lemon slices.

flaming lamborghini

makes **2**

glasses **2 warmed martini glasses**

equipment **straws**

2 measures **Kahlúa coffee liqueur**

2 measures **Sambuca**

2 measures **Bailey's Irish Cream**

2 measures **blue Curaçao**

Pour the Kahlúa into 2 warmed martini glasses. Gently float half a measure of Sambuca over the back of a spoon into each glass so that it creates a layer on top.

Pour the Bailey's and blue Curaçao into shot glasses. Next, pour the remaining Sambuca into a warmed wine glass and carefully set it alight. Carefully pour it into the martini glasses.

Pour the Bailey's and Curaçao into the lighted martini glasses at the same time. Serve with straws.

For a Flat Liner, to serve 1, pour ¾ of a measure of tequila gold into a shot glass. Float about 4 drops of Tabasco over the top, then add ¾ of a measure of Sambuca.

rich and creamy

white russian

makes **2**

glasses **2 old-fashioned glasses**

equipment **cocktail shaker, strainer**

12 **cracked ice cubes**
2 measures **vodka**
2 measures **Tia Maria**
2 measures **full-fat milk or double cream**

Put half the cracked ice into a cocktail shaker and put the remaining cracked ice into 2 old-fashioned glasses.

Add the vodka, Tia Maria and milk or cream to the shaker and shake until a frost forms on the outside of the shaker.

Strain over the ice in the glasses and serve.

For a Black Russian, a cocktail with a rich coffee flavour, to serve 1, pour 2 measures of vodka into an old-fashioned glass full of ice, add 1 measure of Kahlúa and stir. Decorate with a chocolate stick, if you like.

tiki treat

makes **2**

glasses **2 hurricane glasses**

equipment **food processor, straws**

crushed ice

1 ripe **mango**, peeled and stoned, plus extra slices to decorate

6 **coconut chunks**

2 measures **coconut cream**

4 measures **aged rum**

2 dashes **lemon juice**

2 teaspoons **caster sugar**

Put a small scoop of crushed ice with all the other ingredients into a food processor or blender and blend until smooth.

Transfer to 2 hurricane glasses, decorate with mango slices and serve with long straws.

For a Serenade, put some ice in a food processor, add 2 measures of white rum, 1 measure of Amaretto di Saronno, 1 measure of coconut cream and 4 measures of pineapple juice. Whiz until blended and pour into 2 highball glasses over ice.

lobster on south beach

makes **2**
glasses **2 highball glasses**
equipment **food processor**

2 measures **white rum**
2 measures **coconut rum**
2 measures **mango purée**
4 measures **mandarin juice**
  (fresh, if possible)
2 measures **coconut cream**
8 **pineapple chunks**
crushed ice

To decorate
pineapple leaves
mango slices

Put the white and coconut rums, mango purée, mandarin juice, coconut cream and pineapple chunks into a food processor with some crushed ice and blend.

Transfer to 2 large highball glasses, decorate with pineapple leaves and mango slices and serve.

For a Piña Colada, a world-famous cocktail, which was created by a bartender in Puerto Rico in 1957, put 2 measures of white rum, 4 measures of coconut cream and 4 measures of pineapple juice in a cocktail shaker. Shake lightly, then strain into 2 highball glasses, decorate with a slice of orange and serve.

after dark crush

makes **2**
glasses **2 highball glasses**
equipment **straws, cocktail
  sticks**

crushed ice
4 measures **Barbadian rum**
1 measure **Koko Kanu
  (coconut rum)**
1 measure **vanilla syrup**
2 measures **coconut cream**
soda water, to top up
maraschino cherries,
  to decorate

Fill 2 highball glasses with crushed ice, then add, one by one in order, the two rums, vanilla syrup and coconut cream.

Stir and top up with soda water. Add more ice, decorate with cherries and serve with long straws.

For an El Dorado, put 2 measures of white rum, 2 measures of advocaat and 2 measures of white crème de cacao in a shaker with plenty of ice. Shake well, then strain over ice into 2 chilled martini glasses. To serve, decorate with a sprinkling of grated coconut.

berlin blonde

makes **2**

glasses **2 chilled martini glasses**

equipment **cocktail shaker, strainer, cocktail sticks**

2 measures **dark rum**
2 measures **Cointreau**
2 measures **double cream**
ice cubes

To decorate
ground cinnamon
maraschino cherries

Pour the rum, Cointreau and cream into a cocktail shaker, add 8–10 ice cubes and shake.

Double-strain into 2 chilled martini glasses, decorate each glass with a sprinkling of ground cinnamon and some cherries and serve.

For an Absolut Wonder, dip the moistened rim of 2 chilled martini glasses into some drinking chocolate powder. Shake 6 measures of Absolut Vanilla vodka with 2 measures of white chocolate liqueur. Strain into the glasses and drop a cherry into each one.

north pole

makes **2**

glasses **2 martini glasses**

equipment **cocktail shaker**

2 measures **gin**

1 measure **lemon juice**

1 measure **maraschino liqueur**

2 **egg whites**

ice cubes

Put the gin, lemon juice, maraschino and egg whites into a cocktail shaker, add 8–10 ice cubes and shake well.

Strain into 2 martini glasses and serve.

For a Crossbow, dip the moistened rim of 2 chilled martini glasses into some drinking chocolate powder. Shake together 1 measure of gin, 1 measure of crème de cacao and 1 measure of Cointreau with plenty of ice and pour into the chilled glasses.

zoom

makes **2**

glasses **2 old-fashioned glasses**

equipment **cocktail shaker, strainer**

ice cubes

4 measures **Scotch whisky**

2 teaspoons **clear honey**

2 measures **chilled water**

2 measures **single cream**

Put 8–10 ice cubes into a cocktail shaker, add the whisky, honey, chilled water and cream and shake well.

Strain into 2 old-fashioned glasses and serve at once.

For a Silky Pin, fill 2 old-fashioned glasses with ice and add 1 measure of Scotch whisky and 1 measure of Drambuie to each one. Stir and serve.

silk stocking

makes **2**

glasses **2 chilled martini glasses**

equipment **cocktail shaker, strainer**

drinking chocolate powder

1½ measures **tequila**

1½ measures **white crème de cacao**

7 measures **single cream**

4 teaspoons **grenadine**

ice cubes

Dampen the rim of 2 chilled martini glasses and dip them into the drinking chocolate powder.

Pour the tequila, crème de cacao, cream and grenadine into a cocktail shaker and add 8–10 ice cubes. Shake vigorously for 10 seconds, then strain into the chilled martini glasses.

For a Sombrero, make a Silk Stocking but without the grenadine. Decorate with some grated nutmeg before serving.

mexican bulldog

makes **2**
glasses **2 highball glasses**

ice cubes
1½ measures **tequila**
1½ measures **Kahlúa coffee
liqueur**
2½ measures **single cream**
7 measures **cola**
drinking chocolate powder,
to decorate

Put 4–6 ice cubes in 2 highball glasses. Pour in the
tequila, Kahlúa and cream, then top up with the cola.

Stir gently, sprinkle with drinking chocolate powder
and serve.

For a Brave Bull, which packs more of a punch, fill
an old-fashioned glass with ice cubes, then add equal
measures of tequila and Kahlúa.

alexander baby

makes **2**
glasses **2 chilled martini glasses**
equipment **cocktail shaker, strainer**

8–10 **ice cubes**
4 measures **dark rum**
2 measures **crème de cacao**
1 measure **double cream**
grated nutmeg

Put the ice cubes into a cocktail shaker and add the rum, crème de cacao and cream.

Shake and strain into 2 chilled martini glasses. Sprinkle a little grated nutmeg over each glass and serve.

For a Frostbite, shake 2 measures of tequila, 2 measures of double cream, 2 measures of crème de cacao and 1 measure of crème de menthe with plenty of ice. Strain into 2 chilled martini glasses and decorate with drinking chocolate powder.

jaffa

makes **2**

glasses **2 chilled martini glasses**

equipment **cocktail shaker, strainer**

ice cubes
2 measures **brandy**
2 measures **dark crème de cacao**
2 measures **single cream**
1 measure **Mandarine Napoléon**
4 dashes **orange bitters**
orange-flavoured chocolate shavings, to decorate

Half-fill a cocktail shaker with ice cubes. Add the remaining ingredients and shake until a frost forms on the outside of the shaker.

Strain into 2 chilled martini glasses, decorate with orange-flavoured chocolate shavings and serve.

For a Brandy Alexander, a sweet and creamy after-dinner cocktail, shake together 2 measures each of brandy, dark crème de cacao and single cream. Strain into chilled martini glasses and decorate with some crumbled chocolate flake.

x-rated milkshake

makes **2**
glasses **2 hurricane glasses**
equipment **food processor**

2 measures **Frangelico
 hazelnut liqueur**
2 measures **Bailey's Irish
 Cream**
2 measures **single cream**
2 measures **dark crème de
 cacao**
1 measure **clear honey**
8 **strawberries**
1 small **banana**
crushed ice
2 measures **chocolate sauce**,
 to decorate

Put the Frangelico, Bailey's, cream, crème de cacao, honey, strawberries and banana in a food processor or blender with some crushed ice and blend until slushy.

Decorate the inside of 2 large hurricane glasses with chocolate sauce and pour in the drink.

For a Toblerone, reduce the honey to 2 teaspoons and omit the strawberries and banana. Whiz together in a blender and serve decorated with chocolate shavings.

grasshopper

makes **2**
glasses **2 martini glasses**
equipment **bar spoon**

2 measures **crème de cacao**
2 measures **crème de
  menthe**
mint sprigs, to decorate

Pour the crème de cacao into 2 martini glasses.

Using the back of a bar spoon, float the crème de menthe over the crème de cacao to create a separate layer. Decorate with mint sprigs and serve.

For a Banshee, which is really an alcoholic banana milkshake, shake together 2 measures of crème de cacao with 2 measures of crème de banane, 2 measures of single cream and plenty of crushed ice, then strain into 2 chilled martini glasses.

sensational
shots

poppy

makes **2**
glasses **2 shot glasses**
equipment **cocktail shaker,
   strainer**

ice cubes
1½ measures **vodka**
2 dashes **Chambord**
2 teaspoons **pineapple purée**

Put some ice cubes into a cocktail shaker, add the vodka, Chambord and pineapple purée and shake briefly.

Strain into 2 shot glasses and serve.

For an Absinthe Minded, to serve 1, mix 2 measures of absinthe, a generous dash each of lemon juice and Chambord with plenty of ice in a cocktail shaker. Shake briefly and strain into a chilled shot glass.

lemon drop

makes **2**
glasses **2 shot glasses**
equipment **cocktail shaker, strainer**

ice cubes
1½ measures **lemon vodka**
1½ measures **Limoncello**
1 dash **lemon juice**
1 dash **lime cordial**

Put some ice cubes into a cocktail shaker, add the lemon vodka, Limoncello, lemon juice and lime cordial and shake briefly.

Strain into 2 shot glasses and serve.

For a Legal High, another citrus-flavoured shot, muddle 2 wedges of grapefruit with a generous dash of Amaretto di Saronno in a cocktail shaker, add 2 measures of hemp vodka and plenty of ice. Shake briefly and strain into 2 shot glasses.

mint zing ting

makes **2**
glasses **2 chilled shot glasses**
equipment **muddling stick, cocktail shaker, strainer**

2 **lime wedges**
4 **mint leaves**
2 dashes **sugar syrup**
2 measures **apple-flavoured vodka**
ice cubes
cucumber strips, to decorate

Muddle the lime wedges, mint and sugar syrup in the bottom of a cocktail shaker, then add the vodka and some ice cubes. Shake briefly.

Strain into 2 chilled shot glasses, decorate with cucumber strips and serve.

For a Strawberry Fields, another fruity shot, to serve 1, muddle 2 lime wedges with a generous dash of strawberry syrup and 2 hulled strawberries in the bottom of a cocktail shaker. Add 2 measures of blackcurrant vodka and some ice, then shake and strain into a shot glass.

spiced berry

makes **2**

glasses **2 chilled shot glasses**

equipment **cocktail shaker, strainer**

ice cubes

2 measures **Morgan Spiced rum**

2 dashes **lime juice**

2 dashes **raspberry purée**

2 dashes **sugar syrup**

raspberries, to decorate

Put some ice cubes into a cocktail shaker, pour over the rum, lime juice, raspberry purée and sugar syrup and shake briefly.

Strain into 2 chilled shot glasses, decorate with raspberries and serve.

For a Little Last, a gorgeous mix of gin, lime and raspberry, squeeze the juice from half a lime into a cocktail shaker and add 1 measure of gin, a generous dash each of Chambord and sugar syrup and plenty of ice. Shake briefly, then strain into 2 shot glasses.

tequila slammer

makes **2**
glasses **2 shot glasses**

2 measures **tequila gold**
2 measures chilled
   Champagne

Pour the tequila into 2 shot glasses. Slowly top up with chilled Champagne.

Cover the top of the glass with the palm of your hand to seal the contents inside and grip it with your fingers. Briskly pick up the glass and slam it down on a surface to make the drink fizz. Quickly gulp it down in one, while it's still fizzing.

For The Raft, another slammer, combine 2 measures each of vodka and bitter lemon. Pour them into shot glasses, cover with your hand and slam down 3 times. Drink while it's still fizzing.

passion spawn

makes **2**
glasses **2 chilled shot
  glasses**
equipment **cocktail shaker,
  strainer**

ice cubes
2 measures **silver tequila**
2 dashes **Triple Sec**
2 dashes **lime juice**
2 **passion fruit**

Put some ice cubes in a cocktail shaker, add the tequila, Triple Sec and lime juice and shake well.

Strain into 2 chilled shot glasses. Cut the passion fruit in half and squeeze the pulp over the shots before serving.

For a Raspberry Beret, pour ½ measure of crème de cacao into each shot glass, then float 1 measure of gold tequila over the top and slowly lower in a raspberry so that it floats between the tequila and crème de cacao.

fireball

makes **2**
glasses **2 shot glasses**
equipment **bar spoon**

1 measure **absinthe**
1 measure ice-cold **kümmel**
1 measure **Goldschlager**

Pour half the absinthe into each glass. Using the back of a bar spoon, slowly float the kümmel over the absinthe to form a layer.

Pour the Goldshlager over the kümmel in the same way and serve.

For a Money Shot, pour 1 measure of Jagermeister into each shot glass, then float 1 measure of peppermint liqueur over it.

brain haemorrhage

makes **2**

glasses **2 chilled shot glasses**

equipment **bar spoon**

2 measures **peach schnapps**

2 dashes **Bailey's Irish Cream**

6 drops **grenadine**

Pour the schnapps into 2 chilled shot glasses.

Using the back of a bar spoon, slowly float the Bailey's over the schnapps. Very gently, drop the grenadine on top of the Bailey's; it will gradually ease through this top layer and fall to the bottom of the glass.

For a Slippery Nipple, pour 1 measure of Sambuca into each shot glass, then float ½ measure of Bailey's over it.

b-52

makes **2**
glasses **2 shot glasses**
equipment **bar spoon**

1 measure **Kahlúa coffee liqueur**
1 measure **Bailey's Irish Cream**
1 measure **Grand Marnier**

Pour the Kahlúa into 2 shot glasses.

Using the back of a bar spoon, slowly float the Bailey's over the Kahlúa. Pour the Grand Marnier over the Bailey's in the same way.

For a B-4-12, replace the Kahlúa with Amaretto and the Grand Marnier with blackcurrant vodka to make this popular layered shot.

cowgirl

makes **2**
glasses **2 shot glasses**
equipment **bar spoon**

2 measures chilled **peach schnapps**
1 measure **Bailey's Irish Cream**
peach wedges

Pour the chilled schnapps into 2 shot glasses, then, using the back of a bar spoon, slowly float the Bailey's on top.

Place a peach wedge on the rim of each glass, to be eaten after the shot has been drunk.

For a Cowboy, use butterscotch schnapps instead of the peach and serve without the peach wedges.

papa g

makes **2**

glasses **2 shot glasses**

equipment **cocktail shaker, strainer**

ice cubes

2 measures **Amaretto di Saronno**

2 dashes **lemon juice**

2 dashes **sugar syrup**

2 drops **Angostura bitters**

Put some ice cubes in a cocktail shaker, add the other ingredients and shake briefly.

Strain into 2 shot glasses and serve.

For a Kamikaze, mix 2 measures of vodka, 2 measures of Cointreau and 1 measure of lemon juice with plenty of ice in a cocktail shaker. Shake briefly then strain into 2 shot glasses.

dash love

makes **2**
glasses **2 shot glasses**
equipment **bar spoon**

4 teaspoons **light crème de
  cacao**
1½ measures **chilled tequila**
4–6 drops **raspberry purée**

Pour the crème de cacao into 2 shot glasses.

Using the back of a bar spoon, slowly float the chilled tequila over the crème de cacao. Carefully add the raspberry purée to the surface of the liquid — it should sink and then float midway.

For a Tequila Shot, said by some to be the only correct way to drink tequila, pour 1 measure of tequila gold into a shot glass, lick a pinch of salt from your hand, swallow the Tequila Shot in a single gulp, then bite on a lemon wedge.

fifth avenue

makes **2**
glasses **2 shot glasses**
equipment **bar spoon**

2 measures **brown crème de cacao**
2 measures **apricot brandy**
2 measures **single cream**

Pour the crème de cacao into 2 straight-sided shot glasses.

Using the back of a bar spoon, slowly float the apricot brandy over the crème de cacao. Pour the cream over the apricot brandy in the same way.

For an Angel's Kiss, layer the ingredients in each glass in the same way by pouring them over a bar spoon: start with ½ measure of crème de cacao, then ½ measure of brandy and finally some lightly whipped double cream.

deaf knees

makes **2**
glasses **2 shot glasses**
equipment **bar spoon**

1 measure **chocolate schnapps**
1 measure **crème de menthe**
1 measure **Grand Marnier**

Pour the chocolate schnapps into 2 shot glasses.

Using the back of a bar spoon, slowly float the crème de menthe over the schnapps.

Pour the Grand Marnier over the crème de menthe in the same way.

For a Pillow Talk, pour ½ measure of chilled strawberry vodka into each shot glass, then float ½ measure of Mozart white chocolate liqueur over it, followed by a dash of aerosol cream.

index

acknowledgements

Executive Editors: Katy Denny/Jo Lethaby
Senior Editor: Charlotte Macey
Executive Art Editor: Penny Stock
Designer: Cobalt
Photographer: Stephen Conroy
Drinks Stylist: Federico Riezzo
Props Stylist: Liz Hippisley
Production Controller: Carolin Stransky

Special Photography: © Octopus Publishing Group
Limited/Stephen Conroy
Other Photography: © Octopus Publishing Group
Limited 23, 186; /William Lingwood 102, 112, 116,
142, 204, 212; /Neil Marsh 74; /Lis Parsons 8, 13,
94, 106; /William Reavell 170; /William Shaw 76;
Simon Smith 11; /Ian Wallace 48, 80, 122, 150, 162,
166, 188, 198